A TRIP TO THE HARDWARE STORE & OTHER CALAMITIES

QUIRKY ESSAYS FOR QUIRKY PEOPLE BOOK 2

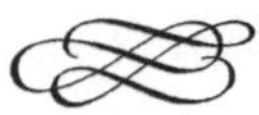

BARBARA VENKATARAMAN

CONTENTS

BOOKS BY BARBARA VENKATARAMAN

Death by Didgeridoo (Jamie Quinn Cozy Mystery #1)

The Case of the Killer Divorce (Jamie Quinn Cozy Mystery #2)

Peril in the Park (Jamie Quinn Cozy Mystery #3)

Engaged in Danger (Jamie Quinn Cozy Mystery #4)

Jeopardy in July (Jamie Quinn Cozy Mystery #5)

Malice in Miami (Jamie Quinn Cozy Mystery #6)

Jamie Quinn Mysteries Box Set: Books 1-3

Jamie Quinn Mysteries Box Set: Books 4-6

Jamie Quinn Mysteries Box Set: Books 1-6

I'm Not Talking About You, Of Course (Quirky Essays for Quirky People #1)

A Trip to the Hardware Store (Quirky Essays for Quirky People #2)

A Smidge of Crazy (Quirky Essays for Quirky People #3)

Teatime with Mrs. Grammar Person

If You'd Just Listened To Me In The First Place

The Fight for Magicallus

Accidental Activist: Justice for the Groveland Four (Co-Author)

A TRIP TO THE HARDWARE STORE

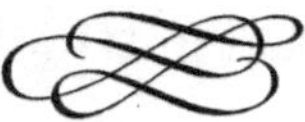

HE ALWAYS GAVE IT HIS BEST WHEN IT CAME TO home repairs, but my dad was in way over his head. The problem was that he wouldn't admit it. Whether it was a leaky faucet or a blown fuse, somehow he always made it worse. Then the experts would be called in, the plumbers and electricians, the plasterers and sprinkler repairmen. Invariably, the first thing they would say is: "Too bad you didn't call sooner, now I have to charge you double." As a result, nothing could get my Mom out of a chair faster than hearing the jangle of keys and my Dad yelling over his shoulder: "Back soon, I'm going to the hardware store." But she was always too late to stop him.

"Not the hardware store!" became a family joke over the years, one that never got old, but no amount of teasing on our part could ever convince my dad to stop trying. The truth is, he would have been happy with just *one* success, one amazing home repair that he could show off and say, with practiced nonchalance: "Oh, that? Yeah, I fixed it myself. Took me no time at all."

Like Charlie Brown, my dad kept trying to kick that football only to have the house yank it away at the last minute, just like Lucy. The most perplexing thing was my dad's crazy optimism that *this* time would be different. Failure was not an option in his mind, but it had become an expectation in ours. We braced ourselves for the worst and, sure enough, one day it arrived...

I awoke that morning to the sound of my sister yelling from inside the shower. Since the shower was just on the other side of the wall, it sounded like she was yelling right in my ear, through a megaphone. It was the worst wake-up call ever, but it turned out she had a good reason for pitching a fit. There was no hot water, not a drop! And with four teenage girls in the house, this was a crisis of epic proportions. This time, we couldn't afford to take any chances. Before my dad knew what hit him, Norman the plumber had been called in to assess the situation.

"Well," Norman said, solemn as a funeral director, "what you have here is a leaky pipe and there's no telling where it's coming from. Could be the size of a pinhole, but that's all it takes. The bottom line is--it's easy to fix, but it's a nightmare to find."

Realizing that *someone* would have to dig up the floor, (and that we couldn't afford for Norman to be that *someone*), my mom made a decision. She knew it wouldn't end well but she had no choice. Turning to my dad, she did the unthinkable. She said, "Arthur, you need to go to the hardware store."

This was his last chance to prove himself and my dad was determined to get it right. Luckily, it wasn't complicated stuff. All he had to do was dig up the floor and find the leak so Norman could fix it, then fill the hole with cement. And, if his daughters didn't suffer more than a few hours of substandard hygiene, he knew he would be a hero.

The logical place to start digging for our underground hot spring was the kitchen, where the floor felt warm under our bare feet. My mom was relieved that the leak seemed so easy to find, but I wasn't convinced. Didn't anyone else remember what Norman said?

Armed with a sledge hammer, my dad attacked the floor with real enthusiasm. It was back-breaking work, but he was a man on a mission. Besides, he wanted to finish in time to watch the Dolphins game that afternoon. Wet chunks of concrete were popping up from the floor like gray popcorn and my dad put his glasses on to protect his eyes. The *bam bam bam* of the sledge hammer was giving me a headache and I had more important things to do, like talk on the phone, and fight with my sisters over the phone, so I went to my room. (Hey kids, in the "old" days, we only had one phone and the six of us had to share it!)

When my dad finally reached the pipe a couple of hours later, we heard him groan. Actually he cursed, but this is a "G" rated story. And, no surprise, the leak wasn't there. Water was flowing INTO the kitchen from somewhere beneath the dining room. My mom started to look concerned about the carpeting. One thing was for sure-- my dad was going to miss the first half of the game.

We were recruited to move the dining room furniture. The only thing we left was the light fixture, hanging in the middle of the room. Under my mom's supervision, my dad gently pulled up the carpeting and padding then continued his path of destruction into the dining room. Thankfully, there was nothing else we could do--except feel sorry for our poor dad. By this time, he had taken off his shirt and sweat was pouring off him. I mean, he hadn't done that much exercise since--well, as long as I'd known him. And certainly not since then either.

Anyway, he kept digging and digging (not really digging, more like smashing) until the entire dining room was a construction site. To give you an idea, there was a giant hole in the floor shaped like Florida: the panhandle was in the kitchen, St. Augustine was near the laundry room and the Keys were starting to encroach into the living room. My dad was so exhausted he was struggling just to lift the sledge hammer. As he hoisted the hammer off the ground and swung it high over his head, we watched in horror as he smashed the overhead light fixture into a million pieces! Showers of glass rained down, most of it lodging in my dad's back. He started bleeding from at least a dozen different places. The room looked like a crime scene! We all rushed to his aid and, after cleaning and bandaging his wounds, we called Norman in for a consultation. Sure enough, Norman spotted the leak through all the debris and mucky water and repaired it in no time.

That hiatus allowed my dad to lick his wounds (I mean that figuratively), replenish his fluids and get dressed because he had to go back to the hardware store (which I assume was no longer his favorite place). I don't know how many bags of cement he had to lug home, but it was a lot, hundreds of pounds' worth. Once he got home, he opened the sliding glass doors to the backyard, removed the screen and pulled the hose into the house so he could mix the cement in a wheelbarrow. The poor guy mixed and shoveled cement for hours. He looked like he was ready to collapse. When he had finally filled the cavernous hole to the top, he smoothed it until it looked like glass. Sorry, painful analogy, he made it as smooth as an ice skating rink after the Zamboni passed over it.

While we were congratulating my dad on his huge accomplishment, Boris (our Bassett Hound who lived outside during the day), made a break for the house. It's not Boris' fault for thinking he was invited in, the door was wide open. You guessed it, Boris ran right across the fresh cement! My dad unleashed all of his pent-up frustration yelling at Boris to get out and poor Boris became so flustered he peed all over the wet cement. My dad had to redo the whole floor.

In the end, we had a funny story, my dad had a project he could be proud of, and my mom never heard about the hardware store again.

DINNER IS SERVED

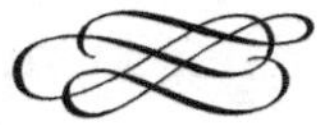

I'D BEEN THINKING ABOUT IT FOR MONTHS, HOW great it would be for all my friends to get to know each other. Then the pieces of my life would fit together like a jigsaw puzzle, or a Dickens novel where all the good, well-intentioned people wind up together at the end. And so I made a plan: I would invite them all to dinner and cook something fabulous. I don't like to brag, but I do have some specialties. Besides, with two cable channels offering cooking shows 24 hours a day, who could ever run out of recipes? I figured that after we polished off a few bottles of wine and a gourmet dinner, new friendships were practically guaranteed.

It took some finagling since we are all busy women, but after dozens of e-mails and texts we finally picked a date. Husbands were put on alert, babysitters were booked, and children were given ultimatums. I had a dinner to plan!

I wanted to start with my favorite salad: romaine lettuce, bleu cheese crumbles, cranberries, candied walnuts and a sesame dressing, but then I remembered: Mai is allergic to sesame and Joette is allergic to walnuts. Unless I wanted to serve Benadryl chasers with the wine and EpiPens as a second course, the salad had to go. Maybe something simpler would work-lettuce, tomatoes, and cucumbers? But no, with Leslie's diverticulitis, she couldn't eat anything with seeds or she'd end up in the hospital for a week...Good thing I remembered!

I decided to give up on salad altogether. Instead, I would serve a crudité platter with carrots and celery and a curry dressing. Done! Wait-not so fast, the curry dressing calls for milk and Monika is lactose-intolerant. Isn't there a brand of lactose-free milk now? Whew! Crisis averted.

For the main dish, I planned to make Macadamia-nut encrusted chicken in orange sauce. Everyone always loves that (especially me) and it's foolproof. Also, it can feed a crowd. Then I realized the sweet orange sauce could cause problems for my diabetic friend. Hmmm...I guess I could omit the orange juice. But what about the vegetarians? There were a couple of those in the group, so I decided to substitute soy nuggets for the chicken. Problem solved. And it could've been worse, they could've been vegans. Or PETA people. Nothing against PETA, but I had no place to stash my leather sofa.

Moving on to the side dish, I wanted to make a yummy casserole that is just to die for. It's called "Soubise," which is French for start licking your lips now. It's made with rice and loads of buttery, sautéed onions (*two pounds* to be exact) and some grated Swiss cheese. Then it is baked to fluffy perfection. Oh rats! My friend Judy can't eat onions, they give her acid reflux. I would have to leave them out.

By the time I started thinking about dessert, I was feeling rather stressed, but I figured if I stayed away from strawberries (because of the seeds) and walnuts, I should be okay. That is, I wouldn't end up killing any of my guests.

The big night arrived and we gathered in my cozy little house. It suddenly occurred to me that maybe this was a bad idea, maybe these women wouldn't like each other at all. I felt like success or failure was riding on me, but I needn't have worried. My wonderful friends were their wonderful selves and by the time we sat down to eat, they had bonded like sisters.

I had worked really hard on my dinner party and wanted it to go well. While I was hoping for a flawless evening, I was willing to settle for a memorable one. And I got my wish. After my guests admired the culinary masterpieces on their plates, they reached for their forks and took a bite. Had they actually been sisters, they couldn't have looked more alike at that moment because they all wore the same stunned expression.

How could food so lovingly prepared taste this awful?

I'll tell you how--by not following the recipes! After I explained the minefield of dietary issues I'd had to navigate, we had a good laugh and decided to order pizza. As I dialed the pizza parlor, this is what I heard:

"No onions on mine, please."

"I need one without cheese..."

"I can't digest peppers because of the seeds."

"Mushrooms make me gag."

"If there's meat anywhere on the pizza, I won't eat it..."

As it turns out, they really were sisters.

LAZY BONES

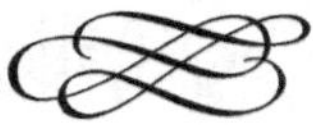

EFFICIENT PEOPLE ARE REALLY LAZY PEOPLE IN *disguise*--true or false? If you said false, you clearly aren't one of us. The truth is we lazies strive to do as little as possible as quickly as possible so we can get back to lazing around. Being efficient fits nicely with our goals and, more importantly, it gets better press.

Case in point: a quick peek at the dictionary reveals that "efficient" means being productive with minimal effort, while "lazy" means requiring little or no effort. See? They're the same. Except, of course, for the synonyms. Oy! If you're lazy, you are *indolent, shiftless and slothful.* Slothful! When the best way to describe you is by invoking the Seven Deadly Sins, you know you're in trouble. On the other hand, if you're efficient, Mr. Roget and his eponymous book can't praise you highly enough. Not only are you energetic and economical, you are also capable and clever, able and accomplished, shrewd and skillful, and also, my personal favorite, *virtuous.*

Not to mention that lazy is often followed by the word "bastard."

So unfair. And where's the gratitude? Where would the rest of you be if *we* hadn't perfected procrastination? Take Hamlet, the biggest procrastinator of all time...okay, not a good example. The thing you need to know is this: procrastinating is an art. A person can dabble in it for years and never become a virtuoso. Only a master procrastinator can leap from the precipice of putting things off into the whitewater of wasted time to swim in the sea of snide remarks without drowning.

Isn't it time the world lauded our contributions to society? Look at our magnificent "Paper Self-Management System" which enables offices everywhere to run smoothly. Also known as "Elimination by Procrastination," this system allows the user to dispose of piles of paperwork without ever touching them. The secret lies in recognizing which documents will take care of themselves without human intervention. It also works with e-mails, texts and voicemails.

Another of our crackerjack accomplishments is "National Procrastination Week." Troubled by the stressful lives of our friends and neighbors, we wanted to show them an easier life--our life, and so we instituted "National Procrastination Week"

(March 4th-10th), to promote the many benefits of putting off until tomorrow everything that needn't be done today. You're welcome.

Of course, I would be remiss if I didn't introduce you to some famous procrastinators in history. First, we have President Woodrow Wilson who prohibited child labor, limited railway workers to an eight hour day, declared war on Germany and wrote fourteen points about something or other. I should probably look that up. I'll do it later, I need a snack first ... oops, where was I? Oh yes, the important thing was Wilson's firm belief that: "Today's greatest labor-saving device is tomorrow."

And then there's Mark Twain, father of American literature and the greatest humorist of his age. He was one of ours. Did you know he changed his name to Mark Twain because it took too darn long to write Samuel Langhorne Clemens? Think of all the time he saved over a lifetime! He even patented several time-saving devices including an "Improvement in Adjustable and Detachable Straps for Garments" (to replace suspenders) and a self-pasting scrapbook featuring pages coated with dried adhesive that only required moistening. Genius!

And talk about efficient, when Twain learned that his birth coincided with the appearance of Halley's Comet, he declared that he would die when it returned. And, of course, he did. His motto was:

"Never put off until tomorrow what you can do the day after tomorrow."

Our third American hero is Les Waas, founder and president of the "Procrastination Club of America." The club boasts 12,000 active members and millions more who are planning to join, but haven't gotten around to it. The club started as a joke when Waas and some friends hung a sign up in a hotel that read: "The procrastination's club meeting has been postponed." Waas has been president for fifty-five years and explains that while the club would like to award an annual "Procrastinator of the Year," they are still waiting for the nominating committee to make a recommendation. (Steel, Piers, Ph.D. The Procrastination Equation. New York: Harper 2010).

So, what are the roots of procrastination? Is this just a modern-day reaction to our perpetual busyness? Excellent questions, glad you asked. Some ancient civilizations did embrace the concept of procrastination. Indian philosophy, for example, gives equal weight to the paths of action and inaction, and one of the foundations of Zen Buddhism is to live in the moment, aware of your actions, thoughts and sensory perceptions.

Hey multi-taskers! Turn off your phones and pay attention. You don't see any Buddhist monks racing around town picking up their dry cleaning and dropping their dog off at the vet, do you? That's because they're serene. They're living in the moment. They're in tune with their inner selves. Nah, they're probably just procrastinating...

The bottom line is: don't feel guilty for procrastinating. The important stuff will get done eventually and the other stuff will take care of itself. It turns out some of the most creative people are the biggest procrastinators. Virginia Woolf wrote in *A Room of One's Own*: "It is in our idleness, in our dreams, that the submerged truth sometimes comes to the top." See? You weren't procrastinating, you were just being creative!

YOUR ACCOUNT IS PAST DUE

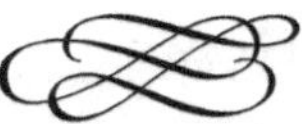

It was bound to happen, but still, it was embarrassing. When you send out as many collection letters as I do, eventually, you'll send one to a friend or acquaintance without realizing it. Oops! Major faux pas...

When people find out I do collection work, they usually give me a look that says, *Oh, you're one of them.* Then they remark that it must be *so unpleasant* to do that sort of work. I pretend to agree because I can't tell them the truth--I enjoy it. And why not? I can make a living chatting with people, listening to their stories, and making deals with them, all from the comfort of home. Usually in my pajamas. Just kidding, I get dressed sometimes. Like on laundry day...

Bill-collecting is a lot like coaching little league: some days, you have to explain the rules, other days, you have to break up a fight or give a pep talk, but it's all good. And like little leaguers, my people have a hazy sense of time, especially when it comes to making a payment plan. Even when the present looks bleak, they're convinced the future will be rosy. They are eternal optimists--but I know better. Although I don't have a crystal ball, I'm pretty sure their lives won't be any different in six months. Except that things could get worse...

I shouldn't give away all my secrets, but my method of bill-collecting requires me to eat a sandwich as part of the process. Allow me to explain. Let's say, someone makes an offer to settle a debt. No matter how good the offer is, I can't accept it without breaking my number one rule which is: *never take the first offer*. Not even if it's for payment in full. Just kidding, I'm a stickler for the rules, but I'm not crazy.

My second rule of collection is to...always...pause at...critical moments in... the negotiation. People hate uncomfortable silences so much that they rush to fill the void-- and wind up outbidding themselves. Without me having to say a word. After listening to their offer, I explain to them that I need to speak with my client. And *that's* when I eat a sandwich--but not while I'm talking to them, that would be rude. The fact is I already know what my clients will accept, so I don't need to call. After lunch is over, I contact the debtor to propose a higher amount, knowing that I can always take less, but this is my last chance to ask for more. And more is better, especially since I get thirty percent. (To clarify, there are times when less is more, but this is not one of them.)

The strangest part of my job is that *I never meet these people.* We talk and correspond, sometimes for years, but I can't put a face with a voice, or picture the guy with the funky handwriting. The sad truth is that I talk to my debtors more than I talk to my relatives, and it's probably the same for them. Not that my debtors are talking to my relatives--what I mean is--oh, never mind...

I can't help it if people want to tell me their life stories. Whatever their motivation is, they sure do some peculiar things, considering that I'm chasing them for money. For example, one woman texts me on every holiday just to wish me a happy holiday. Another sends me her checks wrapped in a piece of paper she signs, "Hugs, Phyllis." Still other people send me notes thanking me for my patience and understanding. *My husband claims I write these notes myself, but it's just not true. If I'd written them, I would have been much more effusive...*

Some of the stories I hear are truly unbelievable and when I say stories, I mean excuses for not paying. Some are tragic, of course, and I am sympathetic to those people. All I can do is tell my client what's going on and recommend that they write off the debt. The other stories I hear are more tragi-comic. Here are some of my favorites:

-I can't pay right now because a trailer flew across the turnpike during the last storm and slammed into my house.

-I can't pay this week because my girlfriend stabbed me and I just got out of the hospital. Also, I ran out of checks.

-You don't scare me, I've been to prison. (BTW, he *is* paying, and I didn't do anything to scare him)

And my favorite excuse of all time:

-Sorry I haven't paid, but I was in a bad accident--didn't you hear about it? My car went off the road into a canal swarming with alligators during mating season and I barely escaped! I was in the hospital so long I lost my job. Now, I've been diagnosed with PTSD and I'm also *deathly* afraid of alligators, but I can honestly say it was the best thing that ever happened to me. I'm so grateful to be alive! I love my life, and I love my kids and even my annoying friends don't seem so annoying anymore. I promise you I will pay this debt,

Amazingly, she did pay it off three months later, so I assume she got a job--maybe as a motivational speaker. All I know is she's my official winner, at least until someone can top *that* story...

And now I have a confession to make: I really like my debtors, even the quirky ones. Take Bill, for example. When his checks wouldn't arrive on time, and they never did, I would call him. He always knew it was me, so instead of saying "hello," he would answer the phone by saying: "I SWEAR to you, the check is in the mail." I would sigh to convey my deep disappointment and say, "Bill, you're killing me, do you know that?" Then we would both laugh and I'd get the check two days later.

Another debtor I'll never forget kept promising to pay but didn't, and eventually I gave up on him. *Two years later*, he sent me a check for the full amount with a note that said, "Here's the money I owe, sorry it took so long."

I ask you, why can't I instill that kind of guilt in my kids?

Then there was Darlene. Her husband was stationed in Iraq and she was just trying to make ends meet. Before sending a payment, she would call first and I always remembered to ask about her husband. She finished paying the debt before her husband returned. Now I'll never know if he made it home.

And poor Vinnie owed money to my friend Kay. Their kids played football together and it always made Kay mad to see him, knowing he owed her money. She didn't realize how embarrassed he was to see her because he didn't have the money to pay.

But the one who made me laugh was Mike. After making a payment plan, he had the chutzpah to ask if I would call and remind him every month.

I said, "Not unless you're planning to send me a Mother's Day card."

He only hesitated a second before answering, "Sure, I can do that."

My faux pas...I forgot about rule number three: Don't be sarcastic, it will only get you in trouble.

And I can tell you, it doesn't work with little leaguers either.

GADGET GIRL

IF THE OPPOSITE OF "HOARDER" IS A PERSON WHO despises clutter, knick-knacks, gewgaws and tchotchkes, then I am that person, with one notable exception. Although I worship Minimalism as a philosophy, and also as a house-cleaning technique, I admit I have a weakness: I love gadgets–specifically, kitchen gadgets. I can't help it. While I can easily ignore the siren call of an infomercial (Seal in flavor! Juice it! Grill away fat!) and I've never purchased a Ginsu knife (who wants to cut their sneakers in half?), I just can't resist a cool gadget. Maybe it's the way they solve problems I didn't know I had, but my online dictionary got it right, a gadget really is an "ingenious device."

Let's start low-tech with the *apple slicer*. Now, tell me this: who wouldn't enjoy eating a crisp Fuji,

Gala or Granny Smith apple cut into eight perfectly symmetrical slices? Nobody, that's who. When Eve took a bite of her first apple, she had to be wondering, "Isn't there an easier way to eat this thing?" She would have appreciated the apple slicer.

Of course, if you want to bake your apple, you should put away the slicer and take out your *apple corer*. Once that pesky core is gone, you can fill your apple with yummy deliciousness like honey, raisins & cinnamon, and then top it off with vanilla ice cream when it's baked. See what you've been missing? Luckily, both of these gadgets are inexpensive and fit neatly in your kitchen drawer.

Things start to get tricky if you're a garlic-lover, and honestly, who isn't? The first gadget you'll need is a *garlic keeper* so your garlic stays fresh as a daisy, er, just fresh. Next up, you'll want to buy a *garlic roaster* because-- what's the point of eating fresh-baked, crusty bread if there's no roasted garlic to spread on it? You'll need only a few more gadgets to complete your set: a *garlic peeler*, a *garlic press*, a *garlic slicer*, a *garlic dicer* and a *magic soap bar made of stainless steel* to take away the garlic smell. Personally, I enjoy the smell of garlic. I'd like to create a garlic perfume called "Delicioso." A light spritz would make you smell like a world-class chef and, in the event of a culinary crisis, you could also spray it on your food. All of these gadgets are essential, but don't worry, they won't take up much space, only half of a kitchen drawer.

Since you still have some room in the drawer, you should consider adding these beauties: a *tomato stem remover, a corn stripper, a lemon zester, a grapefruit segmenter, an herb snipper with a stem stripper, an avocado slicer, a strawberry huller, a cherry pitter, an olive stuffer, a ravioli stamper, a calzone mold,* and my absolute favorite, an *egg-cuber,* so you can make square hard-boiled eggs that won't roll off your plate. Genius!

Now that your drawer is full, let's talk about the fun stuff. You can't live without a *Popsicle maker* if you have kids--that's a fact—and you just can't beat the smell of fresh bread wafting from your *automatic bread maker.* If you pour the ingredients in at night and set the timer, you'll be dreaming you live in a bakery as you bake fresh bread in your sleep. If you're health-conscious, then an *electric yogurt-maker* is perfect for you, and you can always beat the summer heat with your *electric ice-cream maker.* Think of the exotic flavors you could invent, like bourbon with cornflakes, or candied bacon--you can't find those in the store! And how about those fancy Paninis you can make with your *Panini Press?*

But we aren't done yet! Just think how much you'll enjoy the gentle gurgle of seltzer water flowing from your *Sodastream* and the Belgian waffles you made in your *waffle iron,* not to mention the fries you fried in your *Fry Daddy*, the coffee you ground with your *coffee grinder*, the noodles spiraling out of your *pasta maker* and the perfectly prepped lettuce leaves shooting out of your *salad spinner*. When you're done with all that, you can bathe in your *chocolate fountain*. Isn't life good?

You may be wondering where to put all of these amazing gadgets. It's simple really, just get rid of your knick-knacks, gewgaws and tchotchkes, and any other useless clutter, like dishes, pots & pans, and all the food in your pantry, and you'll have plenty of room for all this neat stuff. Enjoy!

WHERE DID THE TIME GO?

My Tuesdays have gone missing. I only looked away for a second, I swear, but when I turned around, they were gone. So now, it's good-bye to my to-do list, my second cup of coffee and the rigorous exercise program I was just about to start. I even miss my trips to the dry cleaner. Sigh...

Before you panic and hire a security guard to keep an eye on *your* Tuesdays, let me assure you, yours are perfectly safe. Mine was an inside job, and I know the thief all too well. In fact, I've known him all my life. The worst part is that he's not sorry at all. Well, he might be, if he ever figured out it was him, but probably not then either.

You see, it's my dad, and he is starting to lose it. He thinks he's just fine, which tends to complicate matters. At eighty-two, I guess he's entitled to depend on his children more, especially since he's fended for himself until now, but I can't help wishing he'd taken better care of himself along the way. Although he feels fine, he takes a pill for everything and requires the services of a dozen doctors--one for each organ, and a few more for good measure. If that weren't bad enough, each new doctor gives him multiple appoint-ments (like multiples of five), and lab work which is always scheduled for the crack of dawn, on the other side of town.

For the two or three of you still unfamiliar with managed care, let me explain how it works: each ap-pointment and test needs a *separate* referral from the primary doctor. These are given out only on the second day following the third night after a full moon. Also, you have to know the secret password. Got it?

And so, my missing Tuesdays are spent making appointments, begging for referrals and, of course, driving my dad all over the place, including the su-permarket. Here in south Florida, you can always see elderly people at the grocery store during daylight hours. Many of them are shopping with their *middle-aged children* (an oxymoron if I ever heard one), having heated discussions about which cereal to buy and whether they really need cigarettes.

Suddenly, I am one of them...but which one? My vision blurs and I am an old lady. I'm in the cereal aisle arguing with my son. He wants me to buy Fiber

One, but I am demanding Froot Loops, why can't I have Froot Loops? Who does he think he is?

I feel myself hyperventilating and stagger over to the freezer section where I yank open the door and stick my head in the sub-zero air. Hovering above the green beans, I take deep breaths and recite a soothing mantra. My father sees nothing unusual about this and keeps walking.

Feeling calmer, I relinquish the freezer to a woman waiting patiently behind me. She gives me a nod, just as her elderly mother catches up with the cart. She knows my story because she's living it. I track down my father, who has filled the cart with groceries he doesn't need and won't use. He forgot that he eats all of his meals in the dining room of his assisted living facility. Also, he doesn't know how to cook.

Later, we grab a slice of pizza and I tell my dad a joke, which makes him laugh. I honestly can't remember if I've told him that joke before, but since he can't remember either, it works out. As we eat, I notice how much he resembles my grandmother now. At the same time, I realize that we are mirror images of each other--the way we sit, how we hold our pizza. I start to feel dizzy as the past, present, and future spin together, pulling me into a swirling vortex. I long for the cold embrace of the green bean freezer. When my father asks me if I'm alright, I tell him *Yes, I was just having a hot flash...* which isn't actually a lie.

On the drive back to my dad's assisted living facility, I can't help but notice the "Silver Alerts" flashing overhead, warning motorists that a confused old person somehow got a hold of the car keys and took off. Luckily, we took my dad's car away before that happened, but we almost didn't. My sisters and I were so naïve, we actually thought he'd ask for help if he needed it. But he knew exactly what we'd do, so he pretended everything was fine. It took us a year to realize his memory was slipping.

As I drop my dad off, I watch him greet everybody (not by name, of course) and then wander off into the bingo room. Unburdened by memory and unaware of his medical issues, he is carefree. And while he may not remember all of his grandkids' names, he knows he loves them. It's not a bad life, but still, I'm determined to hang onto my memory. I've done some research and found out that the best way to ward off dementia is to be physically active, keep your brain engaged, take complex B vitamins and consume turmeric, the bright orange spice used in curry.

So, I hope you'll excuse me now, but I have to go do some jumping jacks, finish my Sudoku puzzle, gulp down my vitamins and eat some turmeric. I think it would be perfect sprinkled over Froot Loops.

BEYOND BELIEF

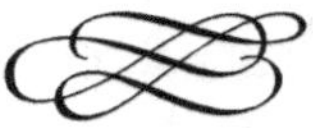

WE WEREN'T MARRIED VERY LONG WHEN MY husband brought it up.

"I can't believe you used to be a waitress."

"Why is that?" I asked, sweeping up broken glass from the kitchen floor.

"Well," he said, trying to be diplomatic, "you drop a lot of stuff."

"So, I'm a klutz," I said. "That's not news. Not grounds for an annulment either, if that's what you're thinking," I said, authoritatively. "Not in this state."

"Not a problem," he said. "*But I still can't believe you were a waitress.* Now I understand why you went to law school, there was nothing you could break. Except the law, of course..."

"You're *hilarious*. Listen, I was a great waitress," I said. "Make some popcorn and I'll tell you all about it.

~

My first foray into the food industry was at McDonald's. I know--that's not waitressing and McDonald's isn't food--but, all the same, the customers were cranky, the bosses were bossy, and I reeked of French fries by the end of the day, so it counts. The most annoying thing was that Lori, my supervisor, would constantly tell me to "look busy." Apparently, I worked too fast for her. No sooner did I finish mopping then she'd tell me to re-mop the clean floor. There was just no point in discussing it. Logic was wasted on her, and humor wasn't a gene she'd been burdened with, so I just kept mopping the clean floor, and waiting on customers, of course.

Another thorny issue for Lori was *suggestive selling,* as in 'Would you like fries with that?' I hated doing it, and she hated me for not doing it. I was passive and she was aggressive, we were the Yin and Yang of McDonald's. Can you imagine me suggestive selling to my clients now? 'I'll prepare your contract right away. And would you like a lawsuit to go with that?' I mean, that would be crazy..."

~

"So, did she fire you?"
"No way! I quit, and I bet Lori cried herself to

sleep over it, too. Anyone can swing a mop, but she'll never find another sparring partner like me.

~

My next waitressing gig was a Chinese Restaurant near my house. I don't remember the name of it and it's long gone, but there was one memorable thing about it--I was the *only* non-Asian employee. I thought I'd be the odd one out hearing Chinese spoken all around me, but I was wrong. While I was definitely an outsider, it wasn't because they were speaking Chinese, no, it was because they were speaking SPANISH and Chinese. They were all from Cuba! If you think "Spanglish" is hard to understand, try "Span-ese" (I just made that up). And the drama! Oh, they had more romance, betrayal, jealousy and intrigue going on there than in a telenovela. But I couldn't figure out any of it, and I wasn't crazy about the food either, so I left.

Which brings me to "Peoples", a chain restaurant with a gigantic salad bar and inexpensive entrees. I think there's one in Texas still, but the one in Florida didn't last long. The thing about Peoples was the food came out *fast* and I really had to hustle to keep up. One day, I was running my legs off when I got seated with yet another table, which put me totally in the weeds. I needed to take their order and then grab my food from the kitchen before the manager saw it sitting there.

Naturally, my new customers, who spoke with a southern drawl, were in no hurry at all. I was stressing out as the couple asked me a zillion questions about every item on the menu. Finally, finally, the husband, a big beefy guy, looks up and says to me, 'I'll have a quickie.' I just stood there, mouth open, pen in midair. The man politely said it again, 'I'd like a quickie, please.' I asked him to *point to the item on the menu.* I was afraid he would start acting it out or something. Turns out he wanted a *quiche.* Clearly, not a popular dish in his home state, if they had them at all.

At the end of that summer, I left for law school. I was dying to get to New Orleans!

Law school was the pits, but New Orleans was so amazing that I didn't mind having to work part-time. The Riverbend Restaurant was upscale, but not too fancy, and it was close to campus. Remember I had just worked at Peoples where speed was not only encouraged, but expected.

During my first week at the Riverbend, I was incredulous at how slowly food came out of the kitchen, so I hung around the cooks asking them *when* was my food coming up. Finally, Miss Adele, the manager, an older woman with big hair, ambled over to me and said, "Honey, let me tell you something. I don't know where you used to work, but our food here does not come out of a can. We cook it by hand and that takes time..." Then she smiled at me and that's the moment I became a real waitress. I still miss that place. I think it got knocked down to build a Winn Dixie...

The next summer I worked for Masa-San Japanese Restaurant, the most fun place I ever worked. It was right next to my parents' office and owned by a man named, you guessed it, Masa-San. My sister Michele and I worked the lunch shift along with a cook who was always hung-over and only spoke Japanese. Michele and I ate Japanese food for breakfast, while Masa and the cook ate doughnuts from down the street. After we made friends with the night shift waiters, we all went bowling together one night, armed only with a Japanese/English dictionary so we could communicate. I don't know what we actually said to each other, but we laughed the whole time. I heard Masa eventually moved back to Japan.

I may have been in a Japanese immersion program by day, but by night I was a cocktail waitress at Victoria Station, a restaurant cleverly constructed to look like three connecting train cars. It was cute, it was fun and it was easy, except for one thing: all of the frozen drinks were served in tall glasses so top-heavy that we worried constantly about spilling them--*especially* me.

One night, it finally happened and in the worst way imaginable. Picture a misstep, a shaky hand and a large frozen strawberry daiquiri with whipped cream toppling off a tray in slow motion, spilling right onto a bald man's head! I'll never forget the tears, the recriminations, the non-stop apologies, and the look on that poor man's face when he got slimed. What a night! I wish that place was still around so I could take you there. And the funniest thing about that daiquiri spilling was that *I wasn't the one who did it....*"

～

"I notice a theme running through your story," my husband said, as he grabbed a handful of popcorn.

"That I'm not as klutzy as you thought?" I asked, smugly.

"No--that every restaurant you ever worked for closed right after you left."

I caught him off-guard when I threw my popcorn at him, but soon it was all-out war with a snowstorm of popcorn flying through the air. Luckily, we hadn't buttered it. After I took out the broom for the second time that night, my husband asked, "Hey, do you want to go for a walk? We could use the exercise."

I kicked back in my comfy recliner. La-Z-Boys are for girls too, although they don't like to advertise it.

"Nah, I'd rather watch TV," I said, picking up the remote. "By the way, did I ever tell you I used to be an aerobics instructor?"

HIGH FINANCE

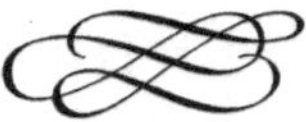

My sisters and I call it "High Finance," but there's nothing high-end about it and honestly, even we don't understand it. Our system is so complicated, so convoluted, that it would make a seasoned accountant switch careers-but only after he drank himself into a stupor. The fact is, there's no algorithm or mathematical formula that can explain it--it just works. And although high finance can be as elusive and ephemeral as a fleeting thought, with no logic or reason, it's always there when we need it.

While we're not exactly sure how it started, or why we keep doing it, my sisters and I wouldn't have it any other way. The truth is we enjoy it. It's a game we play with a worthy purpose, and it saves us time. Really, it does. Oh sure, it makes our husbands crazy, but that's just an added bonus. Whenever we say,

"Time for high finance," they roll their eyes, throw up their hands and try to butt in. But we're stubborn women, and quite bossy besides. If they thought they could change us, they should have married someone else.

"Here we go again..." says one brother-in-law.

"Why don't you pool your money or something?" suggests another.

"Good luck with that," says my husband.

"You're just whistling into the wind..." says the fourth one. He's been around the longest.

Listen guys, we know there are easier ways, but this works for us. High Finance serves as our collective memory, a link that gives us another excuse to interact--as if our kids, husbands, pets, and aging father weren't enough. We use 'telegraphese' to get the job done through e-mail, texts, phone calls and, of course, face-to-face contact. After some haggling over the division of labor, ("Come on, I got the last three gifts!") money may change hands, but probably not. We usually hold back on payment, knowing that another event can't be far off. And future transactions could give you a credit, *or even wipe out your debt altogether*, and that is a thing of beauty.

Now, the usual gift-giving obligations are easy to handle and hardly test our formidable skills. Birthdays, anniversaries, December holidays, graduations, Father's Day--these flow like a calm river through our busy lives. And despite having to remember twenty-one birthdays, we are unflappable. It's the other life events that stymie us, the ones that pop up unexpectedly, like when we need baby gifts, get-well bouquets, congratulation cookies or funeral flowers. These make us nuts. Luckily, we know one of us will handle it and that we'll settle up eventually. In this way, we give each other the gift of time, shortening three to-do lists at once, just like that. Then we caretakers can feel taken care of for a change.

I have to admit that it can get mighty confusing at times. Here's a typical scenario. Let's pretend our names are Ella, Bella, Della and Stella.

"Stel-la!"

(Sorry, I couldn't resist, but I bet you sounded *just* like Brando when you read that. I know I did.)

Okay, here goes...

"Hey, you guys each owe me $50 for Dad's birthday," says Ella.

(B, D & S owe E $50)

"Okay, but Bella & Della each owe me $30 for Ella's kid's birthday," says Stella.

(B & D owe S $30)

"I bought the platter for Uncle ________'s funeral, that was $100, and I also picked up cookies for Dad's nurses

**for $40, so you guys owe me $35 each,"
says Della.**

(B, S & E owe D $35)

**Bella says, "Just tell me what I owe
everybody..."**

**And so, after all the numbers are
crunched:**

Stella owes Ella $50

Della owes Ella $15.00

Stella owes Della $5

**Bella owes Ella $50, Stella $30 and
Della $35**

**Stella tells Bella, "Pay what you owe
me to Ella, then I owe her $15."**

**Della tells Bella, "Pay what you owe
me to Ella, then she owes me $20."**

Stella tells Della, just forget the $5.

And so on...

Checks fly back and forth but in the memo part
we always write "Even Steven." That way we know
we've caught up. And if we aren't planning to get together, we might mail the check with a note that says
"Even Steven, love you!"

We come by this craziness honestly, as a legacy
from our mom. She always took care of everyone,
which explains why, when she died, it was standing
room only at her service. Later, as we sorted through

her things and found her address book, we saw phone numbers for gift basket and florist shops in every city we had ever lived in, as well as the cities where our relatives lived. So, it shouldn't surprise you to hear that we bought gift baskets for her hospice nurses...I think Stella took care of that, because Bella got the last thing.

And so, as part of my estate planning, I've decided that, along with my last will and testament, I'm going to leave each of my sisters some money with a note that says, "Even Steven. Love you!" Just in case we don't get a chance to settle up.

Dear reader,

We hope you enjoyed reading *A Trip To The Hardware Store and Other Calamities*. Please take a moment to leave a review, even if it's a short one. Your opinion is important to us.

Discover more books by Barbara Venkataraman at https://www.nextchapter.pub/authors/barbara-venkataraman

Want to know when one of our books is free or discounted? Join the newsletter at http://eepurl.com/bqqB3H

Best regards,
Barbara Venkataraman and the Next Chapter Team

ABOUT THE AUTHOR

Award-winning author Barbara Venkataraman is an attorney in South Florida where she draws inspiration for her books from the daily headlines. She loves connecting with readers through her books and finds a particular kind of joy in a well-turned phrase. In addition to writing fiction, she co-authored *Accidental Activist: Justice for the Groveland Four* with her son Josh Venkataraman about his successful four-year quest to obtain posthumous pardons for The Groveland Four.

A Trip To The Hardware Store & Other Calamities
ISBN: 978-4-86752-335-3
Large Print

Published by
Next Chapter
1-60-20 Minami-Otsuka
170-0005 Toshima-Ku, Tokyo
+818035793528

25th July 2021